ABOUT THIS BOOK • The illustrations for this book were rendered digitally. • This book was edited by Andrea Spooner and designed by Karina Granda. The production was supervised by Virginia Lawther, and the production editor was Marisa Finkelstein. The text was set in Avenir LT Pro and Invention Hunters, and the display type is LunchBox and Rockwell. • Copyright © 2019 by Korwin Briggs • Cover illustration copyright © 2019 by Korwin Briggs. Cover design by Karina Granda. Cover copyright © 2019 by Hachette Book Group, Inc. • Hachette Book Group supports the right to free expression and the value of copyright. The purpose of copyright is to encourage writers and artists to produce the creative works that enrich our culture. • The scanning, uploading, and distribution of this book without permission is a theft of the author's intellectual property. If you would like permission to use material from the book (other than for review purposes), please contact permissions@hbgusa.com. Thank you for your support of the author's rights. • Little, Brown and Company • Hachette Book Group • 1290 Avenue of the Americas, New York, NY 10104 • Visit us at LBYR.com • First Edition: July 2019 • Little, Brown and Company is a division of Hachette Book Group, Inc. The Little, Brown name and logo are trademarks of Hachette Book Group, Inc. • The publisher is not responsible for websites (or their content) that are not owned by the publisher. • Library of Congress Cataloging-in-Publication Data • Names: Briggs, Korwin, author, illustrator. • Title: The Invention Hunters discover how electricity works / written and illustrated by Korwin Briggs. • Description: First edition. | New York ; Boston : Little, Brown and Company, 2019. | Series: Invention Hunters ; 2 | Summary: The Invention Hunters visit a child's home in their flying museum, where they learn how electricity works. • Identifiers: LCCN 2018015430| ISBN 9780316436892 (hardcover) | ISBN 9780316436861 (library edition ebook) | ISBN 9780316436854 (ebook) • Subjects: LCSH: Electricity—Juvenile fiction. | Inventions—Juvenile fiction. | CYAC: Electrictiy—Fiction. | Inventions—Fiction. | LCGFT: Picture books. • Classification: LCC PZ7.1.B7546 II 2019 | DDC [E]—dc23 • LC record available at https://lccn.loc.gov/2018015430 • ISBNs: 978-0-316-43689-2 (hardcover), 978-0-316-43687-8 (ebook), 978-0-316-43685-4 (ebook), 978-0-316-43684-7 (ebook) • Printed in China • 1010 •
10 9 8 7 6 5 4 3 2 1

I'll be back in 15 minutes, okay? And no digging in the flowers!

To Mom & Dad

THE INVENTION HUNTERS

HUNTERS

DISCOVER HOW ELECTRICITY WORKS

Okay, Dad!

Written and illustrated by

KORWIN BRIGGS

LB

LITTLE, BROWN AND COMPANY

NEW YORK BOSTON

Did somebody say DISCOVERY?!

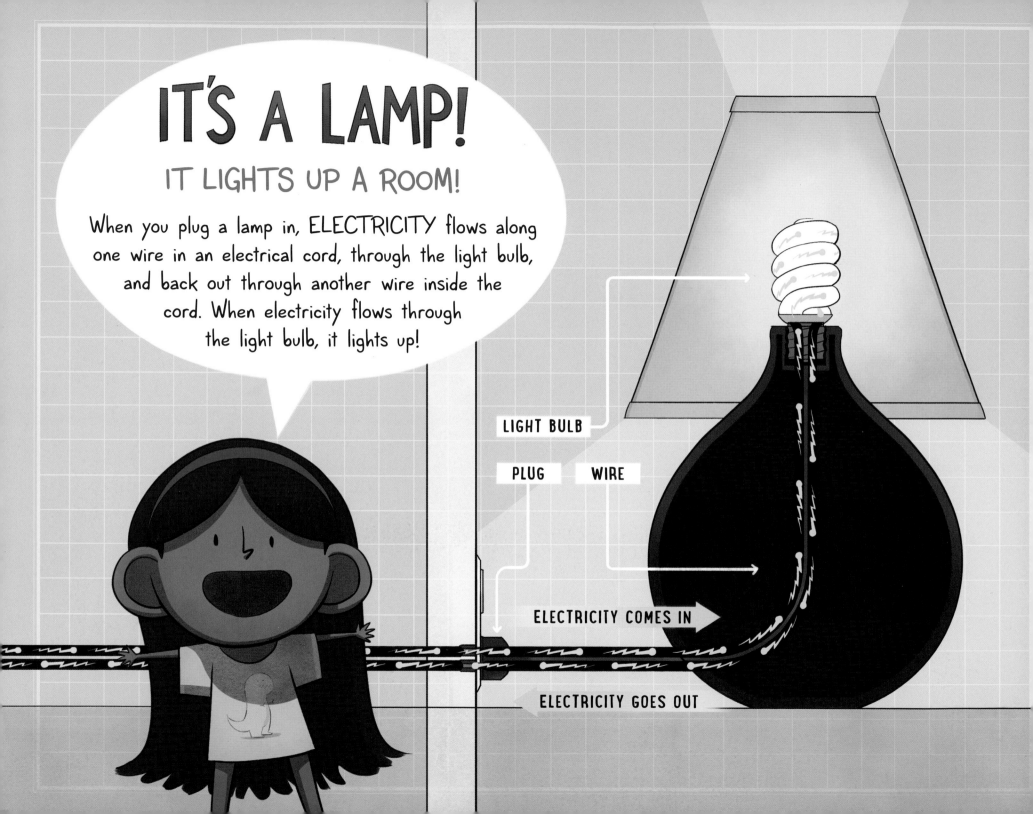

WHAT'S ELECTRICITY?

Electricity is a kind of energy that we use to power things. Where does it come from? Everything in the world is made of tiny particles called **ATOMS**, which contain even tinier parts called **ELECTRONS**. Most of the time, electrons stay within their own atom. But sometimes, they can jump from atom to atom to atom. When they do that, they carry energy called **ELECTRICITY**.

FIRE
Before 11,000 BCE

When prehistoric people needed light, they'd start a fire by hitting rocks together to make a spark or by rubbing sticks together until they got hot enough to burn.

OIL LAMPS
4000 BCE

These ancient lamps burned oil made from plants or animal fat. They could be smelly, and they weren't very bright.

GAS LAMPS
1790s CE

For most of the 1800s, many people used lamps that burned natural gas, an invisible gas that can catch fire. They were very bright, but sometimes they'd explode.

ELECTRIC LAMPS
1870s CE

It took almost a hundred more years to invent an electric light that was bright, cheap, and long-lasting enough to replace gas lamps—the first light bulb!

LIGHT-YEARS!

Most light bulbs stop working after several years, but there's one in California that has never burned out. It's been glowing almost nonstop since 1901!

IT'S A BATTERY!

IT STORES ENERGY!

A battery has a part that lets electrons out, called a NEGATIVE TERMINAL, and another part that pulls electrons in, called a POSITIVE TERMINAL. When you connect those two parts with a wire, the electrons flow through it and power anything they pass along the way.

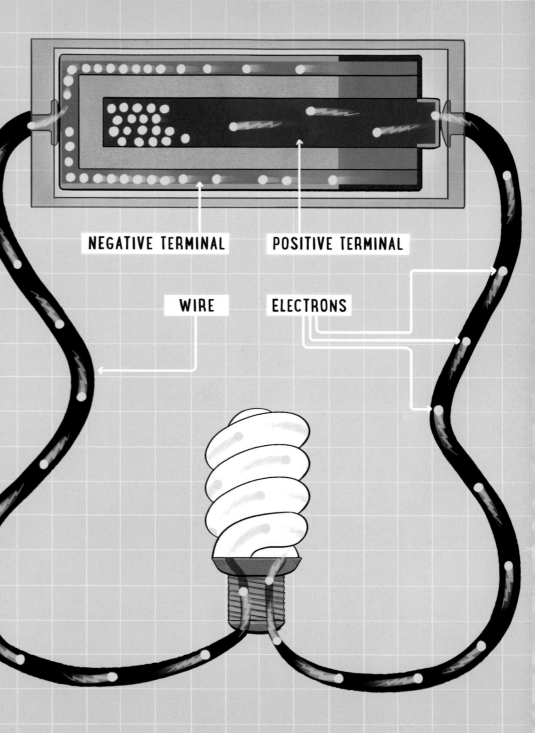

NEGATIVE TERMINAL

POSITIVE TERMINAL

WIRE

ELECTRONS

WHY DO ELECTRONS FLOW?

Electrons like to spread out. If you put something with a lot of electrons in it close to something with very few of them, some will jump from one to the other in the form of a spark. For example, when clouds build up too many electrons, the electrons will zap to the ground as lightning!

ZAP!

IN THE LATE 1700S, a scientist named Luigi Galvani was studying a dead frog attached to a brass hook. When he touched the frog with his metal knife, he was shocked to see its leg move!

Galvani thought that the frog had made electricity. But another scientist, Alessandro Volta, proved that the different metals in the hook and knife had acted like positive and negative terminals, which made electricity flow through the frog's leg. His experiments led to the first modern battery.

LUIGI GALVANI

ALESSANDRO VOLTA

SHOCKING STOCKINGS! Sometimes if you wear socks and shuffle your feet on a rug, you can collect some extra electrons. If you collect enough and then touch a doorknob, you may find that the electrons will jump from your hand to the doorknob and make a spark!

A treasure chest! Let's see what's inside!
It's dangerous to stick your fingers in there!
It's a big shiny tooth! But whose, I wonder?

IT'S A TOASTER!

IT'S FOR HEATING BREAD!

Inside a toaster is a piece of metal called a HEATING ELEMENT. When electricity flows through the heating element, the wire gets hot, and the heat toasts the bread!

WIRE   HEATING ELEMENT   ELECTRICITY   BREAD

HOW CAN ELECTRICITY MAKE THINGS HOT?

Electricity has a harder time flowing through some materials than others. When it has trouble getting through something, part of it turns to heat.

Things that are easy for electricity to flow through are called **CONDUCTORS**. Electrical wires are made out of conductors, so that they can carry more electricity to things that need it.

Things that are hard for electricity to flow through are called **RESISTORS**. Electricity has a tough time pushing through them, and some of its energy turns into heat. The harder it is for electricity to get through, the hotter the object gets. A toaster's heating element is a resistor.

Things that are *almost* impossible for electricity to flow through are called **INSULATORS**. Most electrical wires are wrapped in rubber, which is an insulator. The rubber doesn't get hot because the electricity only flows through the wire inside.

THE FIRST ELECTRIC TOASTERS had nothing covering the heating wires, so it was really easy to burn yourself. Modern toasters are much safer.

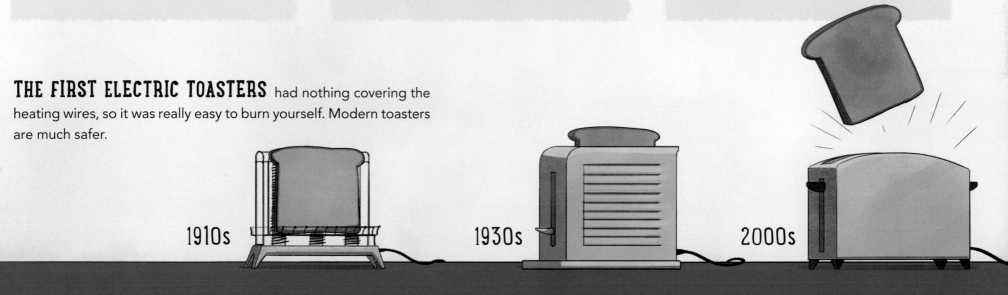

1910s

1930s

2000s

HOTLINE! Have you ever felt a phone get warm while you used it? Even the best conductors resist electricity a little bit, creating heat. It just takes more electricity to warm them up.

THEY'RE MAGNETS!

THEY PULL AND PUSH THINGS!

All magnets have an area around them called a MAGNETIC FIELD. When certain kinds of metals enter that area, a force called MAGNETISM pulls them toward the magnet. The metal and magnet stick to each other, like magic!

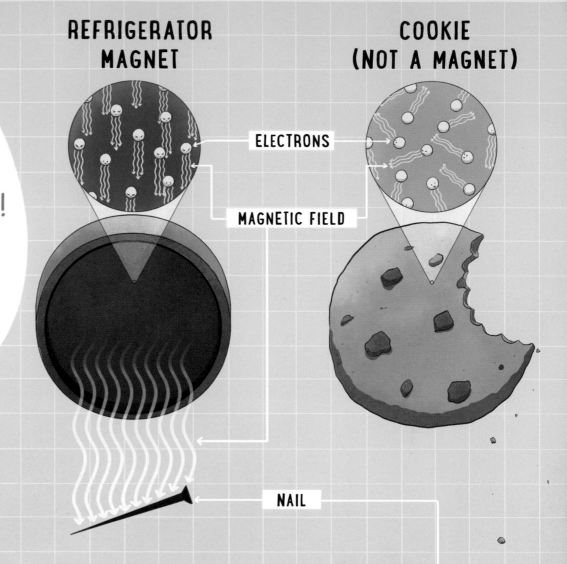

REFRIGERATOR MAGNET

COOKIE (NOT A MAGNET)

ELECTRONS

MAGNETIC FIELD

NAIL

ELECTRONS ARE MAGNETS, TOO!

The electrons in most objects have magnetic fields that point in different directions, so their pulls and pushes balance each other out. But in magnets, so many of the magnetic fields point in the same direction that they combine to make a strong pull.

MAGNET VS. MAGNET

Every magnet has two ends, which we call the **NORTH POLE** and **SOUTH POLE**.

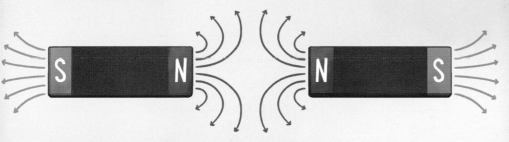

When you put matching ends of two magnets together, their magnetic fields push each other apart.

When you put opposite ends of two magnets together, their magnetic fields pull the magnets together.

WHAT'S THE BIGGEST MAGNET IN THE WORLD?

The world is!

If you dangle a magnet from a string, you'll see it spin around until one end points north and the other points south. That's because Earth itself is a giant magnet! For thousands of years people have used **COMPASSES**, which have spinning magnets in them, to keep track of which way they are going. The magnetic "north pole" isn't in exactly the same spot as Earth's actual North Pole, but they're pretty close.

Where's Santa?

NORTH POLE

TO THE POLE! In most places on Earth, a compass will point to the magnetic north pole.
But if you use a compass while you're ON the magnetic north pole, the needle may point in any direction!

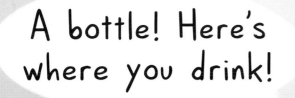

IT'S A HAND-CRANKED FLASHLIGHT!

IT MAKES ITS OWN ELECTRICITY!

When you turn the crank, it spins a magnet around inside a coil of wire. The magnet's magnetic field moves the electrons in the wire, which makes electricity! The electrons are stored in a battery. Later, when you turn on the flashlight, the battery powers the light bulb.

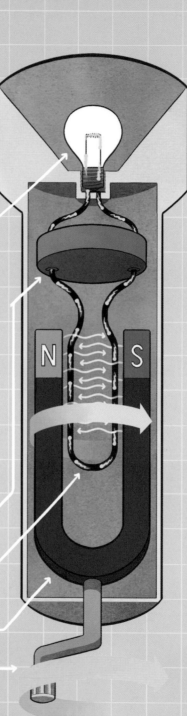

N S

LIGHT BULB

BATTERY

WIRE

MAGNET

CRANK

When you move a magnet next to a wire, it makes the electrons in the wire move, too. And when electrons move, that's electricity!

THE ELECTRICITY IN YOUR HOME probably comes from a power plant, which is like a giant version of a hand-cranked flashlight. It uses **TURBINES**— huge magnets spinning inside enormous coils of wire—to make electricity. Some of the first power plants used a water wheel to turn their magnets.

In a wind power plant, blowing wind turns giant propellers, which turn magnets.

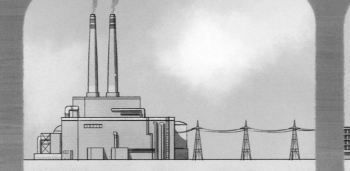

Most power plants burn fuel to boil water into steam. That steam blows propellers, which turn magnets.

Instead of burning fuel, nuclear power plants create heat by breaking apart atoms!

POWERHOUSE!

One of the biggest power plants in the world, the Three Gorges Dam in China, uses turbines as big as houses to power whole cities!

LUMP

A foul-tasting fruit. Displayed with its killer, the two-pronged rubber worm.

ROASTER

Who knows what treasures are hidden inside this mechanical chest? Caution: sometimes hot.